Medical Diagnosis: Burnout

I. M. Tiredoc

Illustrations by Dana Summers

ISBN-13: 978-1976174971
ISBN-10: 197617497X

You may wonder why someone who is already extremely busy and who has occasionally felt burnt out would take on another time consuming project. But when I heard a friend mention that she "resents" her car when it needs gas, there was no way I could let this idea go.

I realize that burnout in the medical field is a serious and growing problem and no laughing matter. Yet, I can recall many occasions when humor helped my colleagues and I get through difficult days. My hope is that this book will have you chuckling a few times as you perhaps recognize yourself or health providers that you know. It's important to be clear that this book is not meant to diagnose or treat burnout; that would require professional consultation. But I do hope that all health providers obtain the care they need to maintain physical and mental well-being.

Why did I decide to use a pseudonym? Well, despite challenges juggling multiple demands of my job, I still enjoy practicing clinical medicine and continue to find my work stimulating and rewarding. I am grateful for my career and the patients with whom I have the pleasure of working.

You know you are
burnt out when . . .

Work

1

When the elevated blood pressure you are warning your patient about is lower than yours.

The most dreaded letters in the English language are RV and U.

You write longer and longer Electronic Medical Record notes that say less and less.

You don't think there is anything wrong with having lunch at 4:30 pm.

You find yourself
envying the grocery
checkout clerks
because their job
doesn't follow
them home.

You forget that although you are on call, *normal* people don't want to be texted or called at 3 am.

Your most dreaded question is "Can you do a peer to peer for insurance approval?"

You cringe when you hear "I need an insurance preauthorization."

You have gone through a lexicon of excuses why you shouldn't when asked "Can you write a note for . . ."

You resent anybody who has asked you for a billable diagnosis.

You see closing out all your notes in the Electronic Medical Record as self-validation.

You have turned down joining a worthwhile committee just because they meet monthly at 7 am.

You don't see why you should write a reference for someone you have not worked with for 15 years.

You don't see why you should write a reference for someone you are currently working with . . . they may be going on to a better job/life.

You don't want to hear "I have this (insert symptom) . . . should I worry?"

You have to force
yourself not to check
email constantly--but
yet you do and
then resent feeling
as though you
have to reply.

Your favorite phrase has become "your poor organization should not be my emergency" . . . in response to every request.

Your resent having to deal with any vague symptoms: what exactly is fatigue?

You crave a week without deadlines.

You justify becoming one of those care providers who looks at the computer and not the patient . . . because you may get home ten minutes earlier

Fun

You think that binge watching House of Cards on Netflix is healthy relaxation.

You have slowed down at work in the late afternoon to avoid meeting friends for dinner.

You have a wellness
program at work . . .
but don't have the
time or energy to take
advantage of it.

You have fallen asleep during every concert and movie you have seen in the past three years.

You have wondered
what jobs would
allow you to work
in your pajamas.

You have wondered if
it's too late for a
career in the NBA.

You look blankly at the menu and can't decide what to order in a restaurant . . . or you order the first thing on the list.

You have texted your colleague at 3:15 in Hawaii . . . as revenge for having to cover while he is away.

You hallucinate about the *Out of Office* email reply you will write . . . and wonder how soon you can legitimately start using it before next week's trip.

You voted against allowing the use of phones during flight.

You worry about traveling to an area with no WIFI or phone access . . . but are secretly delighted.

You have dreaded going on vacation because you have to come back.

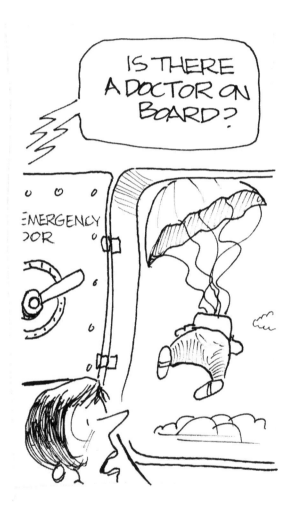

You want to hide
when they call for a
doctor on board.

You are afraid to come back to the mountain of messages after a week away.

You avoid making any non-essential decisions . . . (what restaurant/ bar/movie should we go to?)

Family
and
Friends

When a friend or family member calls, you assume they need something.

Your tires screeched and you left a cloud behind after you have dropped your child at a birthday party.

You have had to gag a child while you answered a page.

When you have reassured your daughter that she looks great as she heads to school with mismatched shoes.

You have forgotten to pick up at least one of your children from someone's house.

You have been asked by your daughter "is there a license for being a parent" when you have been trying to complete your CME and renew your license.

You have felt violent when a stay at home mom shows up to school with a 100 cupcakes and decorations . . . for your child's birthday!

You considered having another child for the maternity leave.

Your family and
friends are afraid
to report any
symptoms . . .
"Unless there's blood,
don't bother me."

You have a calendar
reminder with your
mother's birthday.

You have completed Electronic Medical Record while nursing your baby.

You have bought five years worth of shoes for your children with the goal of saving time . . . and hope that your nine-year-old will still want to wear Thomas sneakers.

You have tried to look embarrassed when another parent congratulates you about your child winning an award at school . . . and you didn't even know about the competition.

You forget all your
principles on child
rearing and decide that
giving your three year
old her own tablet
is not such a
bad idea after all.

You get a visceral reaction when a family member/friend/stranger on a plane says "What should I do about this rash?"

You have had to stop yourself sharing your true feelings when a patient comments on how sweet your children look in their school photos.

When turning the kids
socks inside out
seems as reasonable as
doing laundry.

You have caught yourself saying, "I am on call this weekend" to the checkout clerk as an explanation for buying ten gallons of milk.

You think that gift baskets were created specifically to apologize for being late for child care pick up.

You have dismissed your own child's appendicitis or toxic shock syndrome!

Personal

You reminisce positively of your medical school and talk more of the *good old days* and all the time off you had.

You envy your residents for their 80 hour week restriction.

You are relieved that
the 3 am call is a
wrong number.

You are relieved that
the 3 am call is an
obscene caller.

You talk about retirement with increasing frequency.

You become antisocial on social media: better to keep them guessing if you are doing anything fun, than telling them the truth and eliminating all doubt.

When it's a decision
between exercise
or sleep, sleep
always wins.

You have fallen
asleep at the wheel.

You can't remember
the last time you
sent a hand written
note or letter.

You have driven home and are not sure how you got there.

You have hoped that the niggling right lower quadrant pain is appendicitis, because you could do with a week off.

You have scheduled your C section/ colonoscopy around your clinic dates.

You have stayed in the car when you arrive at work, to delay the inevitable.

Your average night's sleep is less than it takes to charge your phone.

You spend all week dreaming about the weekend and all weekend catching up from the week.

You see a *help wanted* sign in a local cafe/bookstore and consider applying–Oh to be a Barista.

You have not been able to respond *living the dream* without rolling your eyes.

You last saw your own PCP more than five years ago . . . and only because she was your patient!

The best conversation you have all day is with your Uber driver.

You start answering
all calls with "what"
or . . . worse!

You have worn swim trunks or turned scrubs inside out because you haven't had a chance to do laundry.

You are certain you
will be more
relaxed in jail.

You wonder what you have to do to guarantee solitary confinement.

You are happy that you have a balanced diet because you had potato chips and chocolate for dinner last night (vegetables and beans).

You have worn scrubs
to the grocery store
because you haven't
had a chance to
do the laundry.

You have worn a
formal suit to work
because you haven't
had a chance to
do laundry.

You don't think there's anything wrong with replacing all meals with smoothies as a non-chew alternative.

You catch yourself tearing up when watching the Society for the Prevention of Cruelty to Animals (SPCA) commercials on TV.

Even worse, you feel
numb to the SPCA
commercials.

You have ordered your own blood work/X-ray/antibiotics.

Your default answer
to most personal
questions is
"I'm tired."

You resent your car
when it needs gas.

You are too tired
to do the work
survey on burnout.

You have eaten an apple in the hope of keeping patients away.

Your default answer to most personal questions is "I'm fine" . . . but nobody believes you.

You have searched for
*medical license reciprocity
rules Costa Rica.*

You have explained
and tried to justify
how you only need
four hours sleep.

Your idea of fun
is deleting a lot
of old emails
and unsubscribing
from mailing lists.

You notice that you
are wearing a 1995
jingle run T-shirt.

You have normalized symptoms in yourself.

You have gone to your office and managed to nap and resented anyone who called you.

You have bought a lottery ticket, convinced it was going to miraculously improve your life by Sunday morning.

You have looked for a
juggling emoji to use
on your busy days.

In an attempt to dress up, you have spent ten minutes trying to match your hat and scrubs.

You have signed off your voicemail message to your mother with, "Please don't hesitate to contact me if you have any further questions."

You have counted a glass of wine as one of your fruit servings!

You have done some
if not all the things
in this book.

ABOUT THE AUTHOR

I am a practicing physician and continue to enjoy my work and feel incredibly privileged to take care of patients. At the same time, I feel under increasing pressure due to the demands of a changing medical landscape. In conversations with colleagues and friends, I realize that I am not alone in this regard. This project has become a healthy distraction and I am very grateful to everyone who has shared their stories with me.

ABOUT THE ARTIST

Dana Summers is an award winning editorial cartoonist. He also writes and draws two nationally and internationally syndicated comic strips, Bound & Gagged, and The Middletons. He lives in Orlando with his wife Mary Jane and dog, Gracie.

18920392R00090

Made in the USA
Middletown, DE
02 December 2018